No Longer Silent:
Memoirs for My Granddaughter

Aldrena Thirkill

This book is lovingly presented to

Mykhayla Cheyenne Thirkill

by

Aldrena Brenda Pryor Thirkill

First Printing, 2018

ISBN: 978-1-54394-083-1

BookBaby

7905 N. Crescent Blvd

Pennsauken, NJ 08110

http://www.bookbaby.com

TABLE OF CONTENTS

FOREWORD

By Robyn Thirkill

The author of this book is my mother. It is her story. I wanted to take the opportunity to introduce you, the reader, to my mother. She began composing this text as a way to share a memoir with her granddaughter. While writing her story, she invited us to participate. We are a part of her story, yet the book belongs to her. It includes excerpts of more than one story that have not been spoken for a long time. There can be pain associated with speaking truths that have been unheard for so long. There can also be great healing and growth. In our family, I think we tend to focus on the latter.

Knowing your parents as adults is always enlightening. Sister and I observed that our mom mentored many people through the years. When I was a teenager, a gentleman that my mother carpooled to work with wrote a song about her. At the time, I simply did not understand. To me, she was just my mom. I later learned that he depended on her for counsel. He respected her opinions and enjoyed her advice. He looked up to her. They were friends.

Recently, there was a lady from church who would come to see my mother for her good listening skills and expert counsel. The chapter of that woman's life in which she relied on my mother came to a natural end. I do not know what they discussed or which of the world's problems were solved, but I am certain that her life was changed for the better just by sharing a meal or a cup of coffee, because that is who my mother is. I also know that my mother learned something from this young lady as well.

I am not certain, but I think that my sister may have convinced my mother to turn this "memoir for her granddaughter" into a book to be published. However it evolved, we are proud of her for sharing her story and excited for readers to be able to get to know a small portion of who she is and where she is from.

My mother was born on a small farm in Prospect, Virginia. She came of age before and during the civil rights movement and returned post-retirement to the place and church where she grew up. I find it hard to wrap my brain around the fact that we can touch the pre-civil rights era with just one generation. How must it feel to have lived through that and end up back here on the other side? We used to visit Prospect when we were kids and I loved it. My mother also lived through marrying a sailor, raising two girls, and returning to school for her bachelor's degree after retiring from a thirty-five-year stint with the federal government. She raised us in the suburbs, in Northern Virginia. A moderate number of military brats were there at the time, before the big mall and all of the traffic. In hindsight, it was a good place to grow up, a good place to raise a family.

I always joke that my mother came back here to retire, and I am "a part of her retirement plan." Some people have suggested that she came back here to support me and my dreams, but who knows? In my personal life philosophy, I tend to put a lot of emphasis on the path, but in this instance, the destination and my fellow travelers are of the utmost importance. Without my mother and her mother and even her mother, I obviously could not have arrived.

The stories in this memoir are varied. My mother is the only one who could write them, because it is her story. I don't want to go on about how fantastic my mother is, but this memoir offers just a small glimpse at what she has to offer the world. My family and I have had the good fortune to have been able to enjoy her, laugh with her, learn from her, and most importantly, be loved by her for a lifetime. None of us would be who or where we are had she not loved, nurtured, and led us. I truly hope that readers get to experience at least a small part of that good fortune through these words. I know that she has gained insight and knowledge by sharing them.

My mother is a very faithful woman. Whenever people ask about her, I always say, "She will inherit the earth." I decided to look that up and it makes perfect sense.

Blessed are the poor in spirit: for theirs is the kingdom of heaven
Blessed are they that mourn: for they shall be comforted
Blessed are the meek: for they shall inherit the earth
Blessed are they which do hunger and thirst after
righteousness: for they shall be filled
Blessed are the merciful: for they shall obtain mercy
Blessed are the pure in heart: for they shall see God

Matthew 5:3-8 (King James Version)

MYKHAYLA'S FAMILY TREE

Erika Francine Thirkill

Mother

Erik Sweet

Father

Aldrena Pryor Thirkill

Grandmother

Earl (NMN) Thirkill Jr.

Grandfather

Flossie Ligon Pryor

Great-Grandmother

Mattie Lois Buggs

Great-Grandmother

Henry Matau Pryor

Great-Grandfather

Earl (NMN) Thirkill, Sr.

Great-Grandfather

Robyn Arlean Thirkill

Aunt

DEDICATION AND ACKNOWLEDGMENTS

I dedicate this book first and foremost to my granddaughter for inspiring and encouraging me to write my story for her. I give heartfelt thanks to my daughters for their support, patience, and encouragement through my constant questions and "what ifs." Robyn is given a special thank you for the caring and lovely Foreword, and Erika is given special thanks for designing the book cover. I also want to extend a sincere thanks to Terry for editing my drafts and the very special ladies for continuously pushing me to finish this book.

PROLOGUE

Mykhayla, my first and only grandchild, you're beautiful, and I love you unconditionally. I want to give you this book for many different reasons, the most important being that I love you so much and wish you happiness, success, and love. I'm starting these thoughts and wishes with a poem, "You Are Loved," by Judith Bond (1989). However, most of what I will tell you is from my thoughts and memories. The words will not take any particular direction or order, but know that each line is a part of who I am and my love for you.

You are loved
I know sometimes that you may doubt it,
And you may not hear it often enough,
But know this one thing as you walk this earth;
You are loved
Covered with dirt or fresh from your bath,
Respected, rejected, defamed, or acclaimed,
You are loved
You may wear that love proudly as a red flower,
Or keep it silent as cat whiskers,
But, one thing you may never do with that love,
Is doubt it.
This is your guarantee
And your obligation,
Because as surely as you live,
You are loved.

Before you were born, I loved you. When your mom told me she was going to have you, I was shocked, worried, and uncertain about the future. These are all normal and OK feelings. The day you entered into this life was a lovely day. Your mother (Erika), father (Erik), grandfather (Earl), aunt (Robyn), and godmother (Stephanie) went to the hospital. You see, it was a beautiful day for many reasons, but mainly because it was the day of your birth.

I will begin with some information about your grandmother (Aldrena) and your grandfather (Earl), my early years, and what I recall about your grandfather after we met. I will then include papers that I wrote while attending a college that meant a lot to me and at times was very emotional. The papers are entitled "From Bedroom to Flower Garden," "A Time in My Life," "High School Students Walk Out of School," and "No Longer Silent." Then, I will write about my personal challenges and our family as seen through my mind's eye.

I. ABOUT GRANDMOTHER

Birth of Grandmother: Aldrena Brenda Pryor Thirkill

Date: Feb 25, 1948

Place: Prospect, Virginia

Hair Color: Black

Eye Color: Brown

Complexion: Dark brown

Father: Henry Matau Pryor

Mother: Flossie Rebecca Ligon Pryor

Family Resemblances: Father and mother

Brothers and Sisters: Edward (Burden) Legin, (Cora) Arlean Cobbs Jones, Roy Pryor, and

Charles Henry Pryor, Sr.

Story Behind Name: My uncle, Floyd Hill, named me after a girl he met in Germany during World War II

Personality: Quiet, good listener, loner, caregiver, and enjoys giving and helping others

II. ABOUT GRANDFATHER

Birth of Grandfather: Earl Thirkill, Jr.

Date: Aug 7, 1944

Place: Russellville, Alabama

Hair Color: Black

Eye Color: Brown

Complexion: Light brown

Family resemblances: Father

Father: Earl Thirkill, Sr.

Mother: Mattie Lois Buggs

Brother and Sisters: Price Hubbard, Willie Lois Hartwell, Bessie Ford

Story Behind Name: Named after father

Personality: Outgoing; loves reading, sports, and communicating with others

III. GRANDMOTHER'S EARLY MEMORIES

Hometown: Prospect, Virginia, a small, rural town

House: A white, two-story, wood-frame house that my grandparents built. The house had a front porch, and upon entering the house, you'd find stairs immediately on the right that led to the second floor. The front hallway led to a small closet under the stairs and a room to the right that we called the living room. The room on the left was a bedroom, but we called it "the house." I believed it was called "house" because it was the complete living structure my grandparents occupied before additional rooms were added. Continuing straight took you to a step that led to a closed-in back porch. Upon entering the room on the left, you passed a dresser with a mirror, and a right step down led into the dining room and then into the kitchen. In the kitchen, there was a pantry immediately to the right of the entrance. In the right corner, there was a water bucket on a shelf. We did not have indoor plumbing or running water.

Bedroom: When I was little, I slept downstairs in a room with two beds. I slept with my mother in one of the beds, and my grandmother slept in the other. When I got older, I moved to an upstairs bedroom directly over my previous bedroom.

Pets: I didn't have particular pets, but we had dogs and cats on the farm.

School: I attended First Rock Elementary School in Prospect from the first through fifth grades. I went to school in Baltimore, Maryland, from the sixth through eighth grades and then returned home to Prospect to attend Robert Russa Moton High School in Farmville. After high school, I attended Cortez Peters Business School in Washington, D.C., for two years.

After-School Activities: In Prospect, when I wasn't at school, I had to do chores at home such as washing dishes, cleaning the house, and feeding the cats, dogs, chickens, cow, and hogs. Sometimes I cooked and worked in the garden. My after-school activities while attending school in Baltimore were cleaning the kitchen, bedroom, and living room and washing the outside steps. When I left home to attend business school, the life I knew before leaving home changed. My mother struggled and used her house as collateral to get a loan to help pay my tuition, but my everyday needs were my responsibility—food, transportation, books, and recreation. So I had to get a job.

Childhood Ambitions: I wanted to become a social worker, travel, get married, and have a family. After many, many years, I've learned that happiness is an internal entity that comes from within. I have to make myself happy and be happy with who I am.

IV. MY EARLY MEMORIES ABOUT YOUR GRANDFATHER

The information on your grandfather (Earl) will begin when we met, while he was in the U.S. Navy. My roommate introduced him to me. My memory may be a little foggy, but I believe we met at the Bureau of Naval Personnel in Arlington, Virginia. He was born in Russellville, Alabama, to Mattie Lois and Earl Thirkill, Sr. His family later moved to Houston, Texas, where he attended Jack E. Yates High School. After graduation, Earl joined the Navy in December 1961, where he climbed the ranks to Senior Chief. His service in the Navy allowed him to travel to exotic places such as Egypt, Scotland, Ireland, Spain, and Greece.

We married on Feb 13, 1971, at the chapel of Bolling Air Force Base in Washington, D.C. Our reception took place at my apartment in Alexandria, Virginia. My mother and her sisters provided all of the food. I am sure you've heard us talk about how they "put their feet" in all the cooking they prepared that day. The expression "put your foot in it" is mainly used in the African-American communities to compliment a cook, meaning a dish or a meal that is exceptionally well-prepared and tastes extremely good. It can also be a self-compliment to oneself.

During our marriage, we mostly lived in the Washington, D.C., area until your mom was about one year old. Then Earl, being in the Navy, got orders and was assigned to a three-year tour in London, England, and we relocated there. We had to stay in a hotel for a few months until we found a place of our own. Eventually, we found a place to rent in South Ruislip, a suburb of London. He commuted to work in London by way of the subway (or "tube," as they called it there).

After returning from London and being back in the States a few years, he got orders to the USS *Eisenhower*, which was stationed in Norfolk, Virginia. He was very proud of his service on the USS *Eisenhower*, and I recall him telling stories about the indoctrination of sailors crossing the equator for the first time. When a ship crossed the equator, the sailors who had already crossed it had to initiate the sailors who were crossing for the first time. It is a rite-of-passage ritual similar to hazing. The sailors who had already crossed the equator were called "Shellbacks," and the new sailors were called "Pollywogs."

Earl retired after twenty-seven years of honorable service to his country and received numerous awards, including the Joint Service Commendation Medal, the Navy Achievement Medal, the Navy Expeditionary Medal, the Sea Service Deployment Ribbon, the National Defense Service, and the Republic of Vietnam Cross of Gallantry. He was also a lifetime member of the Veterans of Foreign Wars, Post 6396, in New York.

Unfortunately, after being married for twenty-seven years, our marriage ended in divorce in September 1998. However, up until he died, we remained friends and often checked on each other to make sure all was well. Before you were born, Earl moved from Washington, D.C., to Lithonia, Georgia. But he returned to our home in Dale City, Virginia, for your birth. Never doubt that your grandpa loved you very much and always had you in his heart.

Earl had a very kind heart, a friendly community spirit, a sense of humor, and a great love for life. He was an avid reader and had an extraordinary knowledge of world events; he could talk about practically any subject. He also had a great love for football and was a diehard fan of the Washington Redskins.

Below is an early childhood story your mom wrote about your grandpa. I'm sure she has other stories she could tell you.

My Dad Story

By Erika F. Thirkill

My dad had a great sense of humor. Earl T. loved to laugh. However, I did get in trouble with my dad. Often, I was mouthy, and I don't think he appreciated that. One story that sticks out in my mind was the first time I cursed in front of him. This happened during my time of the month, so you know I didn't care!

One day, my mom and dad were sitting in the living room. Mom was sewing or perhaps doing a crossword puzzle. Dad was reading the newspaper. My sister, Robyn, was walking through the living room, approaching the hallway that leads to the kitchen. I came through the front door, barefoot. Little did I know, there was a sewing needle in the carpet. I stepped on it and loudly said, "DAMN IT!"

Robyn stopped dead in her tracks, thinking, "Oh no..." Mom stopped what she was doing and looked at me and then to Dad and then to me again. Dad slowly lowered his paper.

"What did you just say?"

I'm sure Robyn was hoping I'd do the right thing and apologize. Nope! No such thing happened.

"You heard *exactly* what I said!" I retorted. "If you stepped on a sewing needle with your bare feet, I bet you'd say the same thing!" I proceeded to stomp up to my room.

Robyn was thinking, "Aww *naw*, I need to pack her stuff!" Dad asked Mom what was wrong with me, and all Mom could say was, "I think it's that time of the month."

I never got into trouble. I think Dad was just too shocked. Once I calmed down and thought about it, I realized how lucky I was!

*

Below is an early childhood story your aunt wrote about your grandpa. I'm sure she has many other stories she could tell you.

*

My Dad Story

By Robyn A. Thirkill

My parents started splitting up when I was six years old.

I realize now that Mom did most of the heavy lifting in regard to raising my sister and me. Some people might say that my dad wasn't as present as he should have been, but this is my story. He bought me a car (it cost $400.00 and broke down the first time I drove it), and he came to a lot of my karate and basketball events. He managed to be present at as many two-parent events as he could. It was no secret that one of his proudest achievements was raising girls.

As an adult, I realize that my parents were a great example of "uncoupling." It was clear that they cared about each other, and more than anything else, they cared for us. I don't remember ever seeing or hearing them argue, and they remained close friends until my father's death in 2005.

When I was growing up, my father and I spent time together fishing. Fishing was our thing. He would just call me up on Friday nights and tell me to be ready at 4:00 or 5:00 a.m. I didn't mind it as long as we were spending time together. We never caught many fish, but we did a bunch of talking and had a great time.

We frequented a spot near Quantico, Virginia, called Possum Point, a small peninsula in Northern Virginia that juts into Quantico Creek and separates it from the Potomac River. Dominion Power operates a power plant on the peninsula, making the water warm and good for cat fishing.

It was one of our favorite spots because it was frequently quiet, and if you were willing to walk a bit, you could find some nice little beaches. Because the power plant is right on the water, quite a few roads to the water are blocked off with a rope or a chain because they are not meant for public access.

One morning, Dad was convinced that there was excellent fishing down one of these little, forbidden roads. So, we scooted his Monte Carlo around the barrier, drove fifty yards, and promptly got stuck in the mud. We tried everything we could to get the car unstuck and got pretty muddy in the process, but we couldn't do it. Now, we were both stuck *and* trespassing.

My dad left me there while he went for help. I wasn't scared or even slightly nervous. I had the utmost confidence that he would get us out of this. He came back in thirty or forty minutes with a fellow from the power company. The guy looked pretty annoyed, but he used his truck to push us out of the mud.

Soon, we were on our way. I was glad we were free and didn't get into any trouble. I was also wondering if I was going to be able to sneak into the house and change my clothes quickly enough to avoid explaining the day's events to my mom.

Dad had this big smile on his face as we drove off. He explained that he told the man that he had $25.00 in his wallet and that he could have it if he helped us out of a jam.

He gave me a great smile and said, "I had more than $25.00 in my wallet," as if he had just pulled the greatest scam on Earth!

It's all about perspective, I guess.

*

Once, my dad and a few of his retired friends decided to charter a boat and went blue fishing on the Chesapeake Bay. After they had everything arranged, my dad thought, "I've got to have my baby with me," so he got me out of school.

I'm certain his friends hadn't planned on taking any children along, but I didn't care because I was catching fish and I was spending time with my dad.

It was an amazing day—one for the history books. On the way back from the fishing spot, the charter boat guys filleted the fish on the boat, and the seagulls swooped down and ate the skin and guts right out of the air and off the water. I thought that was the coolest. Mom didn't know about that day until I was an adult.

V. GRANDMOTHER'S CHILDHOOD

Darling, my childhood memories are a little hazy, but I'll tell you what I do remember. I recall hearing my mom talk about me being sick as a baby. I had asthma, hay fever, and pneumonia, and at some point, I was hospitalized and not expected to live. The doctors asked my mom if she had any other children and asked her to contact my father because I wasn't going to make it. However, the doctor didn't give up and tried one more thing. Soon, I started to breathe again, and from that point, I began to improve.

Thankfully, I'm here today sharing my story with you.

Growing up, I lived with my mother, grandmother, sister, and brothers. We lived on a farm that provided our everyday needs. We raised chickens and hogs to provide meat and eggs. We had a cow for milk and butter. We kept a garden for fresh vegetables to eat and can. Our primary profit crop was tobacco, but we also planted corn and wheat both for selling and to feed the animals.

We had everyday chores to do, and mine included cleaning the house, cooking, working in the garden, chopping wood, and washing clothes and hanging them out to dry. Because we didn't have indoor plumbing, we drew all of our water from a well. We also caught rainwater for the animals to drink. Also, I cared for my grandmother, who was paralyzed from a stroke, when my mom was away at work. During the summer months, I took care of my niece, nephew, and cousin, too.

I imagine that you might think that it was rough back then, but it was all we knew, and no other way of life existed for us. I had bouts of seasonal hay fever, asthma attacks, and nosebleeds, but overall, it was an OK life.

My father lived in Baltimore so that he could work and provide for his family. I remember Mama sending me there one summer to stay with him for about a week. Daddy lived with my Mama's brother, Uncle Floyd Ligon, and his wife, Aunt Inell (Nell) Ligon. Then I went to New York and stayed with my sister, Arlean Cobb Jones, for about a month.

VI. FROM THE BEDROOM TO
THE FLOWER GARDEN

During the summer of 1959, I was living and working on a farm in the house where I was born and grew up located in Prospect, Virginia. It was a very difficult time for my family. We children had to take on additional responsibilities. My grandmother was the cornerstone of the family, my mother was the head of the household, and each child had various responsibilities including farm work, housework, and chores.

My mother, who was the main caregiver for my grandmother, worked outside the home as a domestic worker. Our days started at dawn with my mother getting up; she put on her robe and slippers, made a fire in the woodstove, and got the coffee ready for brewing. The aroma of the coffee rose upstairs to my bedroom, which told me it was time to get up. To this day, the smell reminds me of an early-morning sunrise.

I stood on the front porch with a hot cup of coffee between my hands, watching the sun crest—a large, burnt-orange sun, rising over the tall autumn trees. I sipped the hot coffee and savored the warm, rich taste: sweet, dark, and creamy, like chocolate flowing slowly down my throat. It warmed my whole body as the morning dew cast a fine mist on my face.

Just after daybreak, when the farm was still moist, my mother mixed up the hogs' breakfast. My brothers took care of the hogs and cow as well as the corn, wheat, and tobacco fields. I was responsible for the indoor chores: cleaning, cooking, washing clothes, and caring for the dogs, cats, and chickens.

A stroke rendered my grandmother paralyzed on her right side, and she was required to use a wheelchair. She loved visiting her flower garden, and my biggest challenge was getting her from her bedroom to her flower garden.

The bedroom had one window that looked out over the front porch. Two full-size beds furnished the room, one by the left wall with the headboard to the left of the window. Grandma's bed was beside the window, with the headboard flush against the right wall. The remaining furniture included a mirrored dresser on the back wall between the door leading to the hallway and door leading to the dining room, a small pot-bellied woodstove in the center-right wall, and a ceiling vent that connected the downstairs and upstairs bedrooms. A mantelpiece above the woodstove held pictures, vases, and an old, wind-up mantel clock that chimed every half hour. There was also an overstuffed chair in the opposite corner on the right wall.

The task of getting Grandma ready to go outside to visit her flower garden required careful planning. First, I helped her sit up on the bed and put her legs on the floor so that I could help her get dressed. Second, I brought in a straight-back chair from the dining room and placed it in front on her. The chair provided additional support to prevent Grandma from falling while I moved to her right side and got her up from a sitting position. Next, I helped her stand, and she held onto the back of the chair and moved away from the bed a little so that her left side was next to the bed. The wheelchair was still placed behind her, and she would sit in the wheelchair using the bed and chair back for support. I then moved the straight-back chair away, and I placed her feet on the wheelchair footrest. Finally, I wheeled Grandma from the bedroom, through the door, down the hall, and out to the front porch. However, to get to the flower garden, we had to maneuver down two small steps on the porch—no easy task.

While I prepared to help her get down, Grandma sat on the porch and enjoyed the view of her flower garden, the warm sun, and sometimes a light breeze. I went back to the bedroom, got the straight-back chair, and placed it on the ground with the back next to the bottom step. I secured the wheelchair and helped Grandma stand so that she could hold onto the back of the chair. Together, we slowly made our way down the steps to the yard. She held onto the chair while I quickly got the wheelchair and placed it behind her so that she could sit.

On rare occasions, Grandma enjoyed being lifted from the bedroom and was content to sit on the porch and take pleasure in the view of the outdoors. Occasionally, a sad expression crossed her face when she thought about her deceased spouse, but within a moment, the brightness returned, and she reminisced about her happy, fulfilled life.

She shared stories about each of her children such as their likes and dislikes, strengths and weaknesses, spouses and children, and her special love for each one of them. For example, through her stories, I re-experienced the delight and joy she felt when the family gathered for special occasions. Everyone had something to do at breakfast: Someone peeled apples, someone made eggs, and someone cooked meat. It all happened under Grandma's watchful eye. She delighted in giving instructions, and we were happy to receive her guidance.

Grandma was serene in her garden. A glimpse of the garden through her eyes was a glorious moment. I saw her walking in the garden with an angelic glow in her eyes, her long, silver hair flowing down her back, and an intimate smile creasing her lips.

God magnified my vision and quieted my soul so that I could see and enjoy this awesome sight. When we were together, the same calm and peacefulness that clustered Grandma's psyche had suspended my being, as if I were in the Garden of Eden.

Grandma was a pillar of our family. She was one of our oldest members and knew virtually every family member's inner strength and beauty. Grandma taught us the true meaning of the simple things in life. For example, she taught me that there is nothing like a clear, starry summer night in the country.

The glow on my grandmother's face and the sparkle in her eyes made our journeys to the garden very rewarding. She sometimes sat for a little while and enjoyed the sights and sounds: the birds flying and chirping, the chickens clucking, the cats meowing, and the dogs barking. The sounds were methodical; the world was listening, bringing music to her ears. She savored the beauty of her surroundings.

Subsequently, she would lean over and pick a few weeds and pieces of grass out of the flower garden. I asked questions about the garden; she would beam, with the same sparkle in her eyes, as she told me different stories about the flowers and plants. One of my favorite stories was about her and Grandpa's relocation from West Virginia to Virginia; Grandma had taken care of her plants and flowers during the trip to ensure that they would not die. During the mid-1900s, my grandparents walked and traveled by train to relocate, and I imagined that she gave great care and attention to plants (and her son, too, of course) during their journey.

On Mother's Day, as it was then and remains the tradition today, the way to honor mothers is to wear a red or white flower: red indicates a living mother and white indicates a deceased mother. Grandma loved to tell the story of the two rose bushes that she planted by the house that bloomed every year in time for Mother's Day. Today, the red rose bush still blooms by the left side of the porch in honor of mothers.

Grandma also reminisced about how she picked the children's favorite flowers on their birthdays and made a special arrangement for them that she put on the table when everyone gathered for the evening meal.

The flower garden, a rainbow of colors that Grandma adored, was a wonderful treat for her. On the front of the porch, she kept a variety of colorful flowers on each side of the steps, and on the right side of her porch was the red rose garden.

On most of our morning journeys, we glided to the right side to catch a glimpse of the green plants and shrubbery. Then, if Grandma was up for it, we took a stroll to the far right corner of the yard to observe the yellow-heart peach tree. It produced small, yellow peaches that we used to make peach preserves and pickled peaches.

At times, we would extend our journey to the back of the house, where there was a rock pile that we used to start fires. We used an oval-shaped iron pot on that fire to make soap. The well was also at the back of the house, and I would often draw a bucket of water so that Grandma could take a cool drink out of the dipper.

The fulfillment of getting Grandma from her bedroom to the front yard was a breathtaking outing for both of us. I gained many valuable lessons from this experience, mostly about working with the elderly, being patient, and enjoying life. Particularly, I learned how to help older individuals face the aging process.

We begin the aging process as soon as we are born, and that process sometimes results in heart disease, blindness, or loss of limbs. However, with years of rich experience and reflection, we can rise above many circumstances that we face. Contrary to what one might assume, old age and physical limits can foster creativity and fulfillment. We all know what aging does to people—how it makes us frail and more likely to succumb to illness—but my grandmother met her limitations with optimism. She was intent on confronting and outwitting any physical or moral obstacle with determination and a "can-do" attitude.

If we view age only as a decline from youth, we make age the problem, and we never face the real problems that keep us from evolving and leading continually useful, vital, and productive lives. The moment you start viewing old age as another stage of potential development in life instead of as a terminal disease, all sorts of promising possibilities present themselves. The delight of being human is that we get old and die. Growing old is what the greatest art is about, and it's what makes the flowers and the sunset beautiful. Fear of aging speeds the very decline we dread most, and it ultimately robs our life of any meaning.

The patience I learned by helping Grandma was instrumental to understanding these things. I learned how to allow her to succeed at her own pace, which gave her a feeling of usefulness. I learned how crucial patience is, which was reinforced throughout being a wife, raising my daughters, and being a part of the workforce.

*

Independently and together, people are constantly exploring ways to improve quality of life. "Conscious Aging is a new way of looking at and experiencing aging that moves beyond our cultural obsession with youth and toward respect for wisdom of old age." (Psychology Today) One primary goal of conscious aging is to change the prevailing view that aging is all bad. Instead, people should consider all aspects of nature, including their advancement through time.

Perspective is a powerful influence on our attitudes and behaviors. If we hold mostly negative views, our interactions will limit our outlooks. Instead, we should try to acquire enough knowledge to promote the care of and respect for senior citizens so that we can understand their strengths and weaknesses. Perspective will increase positive interactions between people of different generations and, hopefully, foster a cultural movement that better appreciates aging.

The education I acquired from taking care of my grandmother was vital to changing my attitude and gave me a better insight on aging. The first step was recognizing the negative feeling that I had within me. We need to be aware of our mindsets to be more positive in our contacts with seniors.

VII. A TIME IN MY LIFE

I was born in 1948 to Flossie Ligon Pryor and Henry Matau Pryor in Prospect during the "baby boom" generation. I attended segregated public schools in Prince Edward County, Virginia. My life crossed paths with several major historical events. The generation born during this period, myself included, had a profound impact on society and the economy. The landmark Supreme Court decision of 1954, which closed the segregated schools, and the March on Washington in 1963 altered the course of my life. I was uprooted from my rural life in Virginia and was sent to the metropolis of Baltimore, Maryland.

I eagerly started school in September 1954 at First Rock Elementary School, where I studied from first through fifth grade. My first-grade teacher, Mrs. Hazel Carter, was also a friend of most of the families in the area. She lived close to our family home. If any of us children did not behave in school, she punished us with a smooth, flat, wooden bat. The misbehaving student held out a hand, and depending on the severity of the crime, she determined how many times she would hit the student. Then, to add insult to injury, she showed up at that student's house before he got home from school to tell his mother about his behavior, which meant more punishment.

Mrs. Carter wrote obituaries by hand and read them at home-going services that were held by our church. She wrote several obituaries for our family members, including my grandfather, grandmother, and a few uncles. Her daughter, her only child, moved her to Pennsylvania to live with her after she got up in age, but they returned for visits periodically. Mrs. Carter lived to be 103 years old and slowed down a little as she approached triple digits, but her mind stayed rather sharp through it all. Mrs. Carter was well-liked in our community and used her knowledge as a teacher to help many people who otherwise had very little access to education.

One portion of the school during this period (1954–1959) was referred to as the "tar paper shack" because it was a single, wood building covered in tar paper. These buildings were erected throughout the area to eliminate overcrowding in schools. They were not ideal; they leaked when it rained, and the woodstove did not warm the entire building in the winter. But we put up with it because we were getting an education.

The 1954 landmark Supreme Court decision, *Brown v. the Board of Education*, ruled that school segregation violated the Constitution of the United States. That decision allowed me to dream of education with improved schools, enhanced textbooks, and anticipation of a better future. Sadly, my vision for better schools ended when the decision was made to close the public schools rather than integrate them in June 1959.

Defiantly, the Prince Edward County Board of Supervisors upheld the Assembly of Virginia Sessions of 1869, in which it was stipulated "that white and colored persons shall not be taught in the same school, but in separate schools." Prince Edward County took a stand of "massive resistance" against the Supreme Court ruling. Consequently, the Board of Supervisors announced its intentions to cease funding of the public school system in Prince Edward County until further notice because they did not want to integrate.

On the last day of school in June 1959, the fifth-grade teacher told us that the schools would not reopen in the fall. I was one of many children who experienced a range of emotions—from disbelief to sadness. We thought that school *had to* reopen in the fall because our parents would get in trouble if they didn't send us to school. I was numb and didn't have the power to think or to feel clearly. I rode home on a bus full of children, and for the first time in five years, every person on that bus was silent. After getting off the bus, I walked home, still in a state of deadness, praying that my mother would help me understand, give me a reason why, and give my life meaning again. At home, Mama had nothing to say. I guess she was as numb as I was.

The school closures created an era of silence. For me, it lasted for over forty years. I did not understand what was happening. No administrators, counselors, teachers, or parents were availed upon to help explain the school closures to children. When the schools did not reopen, our dreams of getting proper educations began to die. I was grieving a life that I would never lead. I thought that because of it, I could never get a job or be successful. I can only imagine what Mama was feeling; she wanted a better life for her children, and this dream had been ripped away from her as well. Mama and other parents thought that the schools would only close for a short time.

The disquiet for my family and me did not end with the closed schools; Grandmother died in November 1959, and my father died in Baltimore in March 1960. Mama and I were there when he passed; he was ill and in the hospital, and we were visiting him. When Mama and I returned to Prince Edward County, we brought his body with us.

Daddy was born in Pamplin, Virginia, and his funeral was held at Sulphur Springs Baptist Church. The course of events—three children out of school, the loss of her mother, and the loss of her husband—was devastating for my mother.

After the first year of school closure, my mother was desperate to find a way to educate her children. So, Roy, Charles, and I, along with several other families from Prospect, rented a house in Appomattox so that we children could attend Carver-Price High School. However, a surveyor determined that the bedrooms in the rented house were in Prince Edward County; therefore, we could not attend school at Carver-Price because we did not live in Appomattox. It was the first semester of the second year of the closing of the schools. Mama was distraught. I imagine that she didn't know what to do next.

Mama asked her brother and his wife if we could live with them and attend school in Baltimore, and they agreed. So, we went to Maryland to live with Uncle Floyd and Aunt Nell. My mama's sister, Estelle Ligon Epperson, and her grandson Willie, who lived with her, also went to Baltimore.

Aunt Estelle went primarily to take care of the four of us—Willie, Roy, Charles, and me. She was also able to take some of the pressure off of Aunt Nell and Uncle Floyd, who was not well from time to time, plus they had a son of their own with Down's syndrome. We got to Baltimore in September 1960, early enough in the semester to get into school without any difficulty.

Some people considered us fortunate; many other children were sent away with total strangers to unknown places to get the chance to attend school. A few families and groups came forward and opened their homes to take children in so that they could continue some form of education. Parents were grateful for the kindness of strangers, but it was a very frightening experience for us children to leave our parents and the lives we knew.

The new setting was most traumatic for me. When you grow up on a farm, and all you know is farm life, a different environment is scary. We traded well water, an outhouse, and woodstoves for electric heat, indoor plumbing, sidewalks, and streetlights. It was very frightening. Nevertheless, the silence continued because I did not know how to deal with all the changes that were taking place. It was as if there was an unspoken rule not to talk or ask questions, only to do as told.

*

I am going to try and share my experience in Baltimore. I say "try" because this is the portion of my life about which I have very little memory.

My reflections during the years 1960 to 1962 escape my memories. I know that I attended school in Baltimore, but I can only recall the place I lived and the way I was treated there. The house had three levels, and we lived on the second floor. I don't remember much of anything about school—not one teacher and hardly any of the other students. I remember one incident when I had to leave school because I had an accident. I remember that a boy and I had both achieved high grades that could've allowed us to advance, but I was lower in math and did not advance with him.

The years I spent in Baltimore were bittersweet because I was obtaining an education but was denied the warmth and comfort of my mother. Mama stayed behind in Prospect to run the farm. With her children gone, Mama had to do everything herself. She made a huge sacrifice to see to it that her kids got educated.

Mama struggled to send money, fresh vegetables, and meat to our house in Baltimore with our uncle and aunts, but the food was not usually shared with us. We ate oatmeal, beans, and hot dogs instead of the fresh farm staples that my mother struggled and sacrificed to provide for us. Most of the good stuff—greens, chicken, ham, eggs, rolls—was eaten by the other, older members of the household, not my brothers and me. My two brothers have the same memories regarding the food. My oldest brother would tell Mama, but Mama always said, "I know it, but I have to send it."

We often caught a ride to Prospect with a relative or someone from Baltimore to visit our mother. On one occasion, a guy friend of mine drove us home to Prospect. Once, on one of our visits home, we decided to go to a drive-in movie. Someone in our car got out to get some refreshments, and apparently, people saw and reported us for being parked in the wrong area. Prince Edward County was segregated and had a Colored parking section and a White parking section. The police asked us to move to the Colored parking section, which had pot-holes and was poorly kept.

My life in 1963 was an emotional whirlwind that impacted my personal life, but it was affecting the rest of the world as well. The civil rights movement was in full swing, and we wanted to be a part of it. When we came home in the summer of 1963, my brothers and I became active in the nonviolent civil rights movement as followers of Dr. Martin Luther King, Jr.

The leaders spread the news about the movement by word of mouth throughout the local churches. Upon learning of the demonstrations, we became an active part of the movement and caught rides into town to attend workshops to learn how to be nonviolent and protect ourselves in the case of an arrest or physical violence. For example, we learned that if we were arrested, we should assume the fetal position—our knees drawn tightly into our chests and our arms placed over our heads. The seasoned people told us, "If you get arrested, just fall and don't fight."

We performed sit-ins at a lunch counter and picketed stores that would not hire people of color. We carried signs by the movie theater and tried to purchase tickets, but they wouldn't sell us any. The "White only" and "Colored only" signs were displayed at water fountains, doctor offices, dentist offices, and hospital waiting rooms.

The demonstrations enabled us to participate in the historic March on Washington for Jobs and Freedom on Aug 28, 1963, where Dr. King delivered his famous "I Have a Dream" speech. During this era, giving one's life in the name of the cause was common, and I was willing and prepared to do so.

I returned home permanently to attend the "free schools" that opened in September of 1963 and was assigned to the ninth grade. The county's public school system reopened as an integrated system after being closed for five years. Everyone was so happy, and hearing the news that we did not have to go back to Baltimore was like having a birthday party. I only recall one White student at my new high school.

The United States Attorney General Robert F. Kennedy honored us with a visit and spoke at a special assembly on May 11, 1964. His wife accompanied him, and I remember when they came down the aisle where I was standing to greet them. Robert R. Moton High School was renamed Prince Edward High School. The former high school is the first school to be designated as a historic landmark, and it is now called the Robert Russa Moton Museum.

According to its website, the mission of the museum "preserves and constructively interprets the history of Civil Rights in Education, specifically as it relates to Prince Edward County and the leading role its citizens played in America's transition from segregation toward integration." Furthermore, to assist persons affected by the schools' closing, the *Brown v. Board of Education* scholarship program was established as Virginia's "redemptive moment." The program was designed to help individuals who are current residents of Virginia to continue the education that was lost to them while the schools were closed.

Despite these changes, the silence continued and was buried deep within my consciousness. I didn't speak about that period. Once, I attended a musical play about that era that stirred something deep within and reminded me of a quote I read by Dr. Martin Luther King, Jr.: "Our lives began to end the day we become silent about the things we know."

IX. HIGH SCHOOL STUDENTS
WALK OUT OF SCHOOL

I explained to you how the Supreme Court's decision and the closing of the schools in Prince Edward County altered the course of my life. Now, I would like to explain the events that helped to bring about much-needed change. On April 23, 1951, 450 students at Robert R. Moton High School in Prince Edward County walked out of school to protest overcrowding and inadequate facilities (Baker W03). They did not envision that this protest would become part of the historic *Brown v. Board of Education of Topeka, Kansas* case that triggered massive resistance by Virginia's governing officials to the Supreme Court decision. Closing public schools in defiance of *Brown* was far beyond their imagination.

The Moton students had grown tired of promises to build a new school to alleviate overcrowding and improve facilities. The high school was built to house 180 students and was close to being overcrowded when it opened in 1939. However, at the time of the student protest in 1951, the building accommodated approximately 450 students (Baker W03). To help with overcrowding, three temporary one-room structures were created from pinewood and covered in heavy black paper (the "tar paper shacks" I told you about before). All but one of the Non-White Schools were constructed from wood, heated by woodstoves, offered only outdoor privies, and had no cafeterias or locker rooms. On the contrary, the White schools were constructed from brick, heated with steam or hot water, and offered cafeterias, locker rooms, and indoor toilets.

The student strike was led by sixteen-year-old Barbara Johns and a few trusted classmates. The students kept their plans of protest a secret out of fear that their parents and teachers would suffer retaliation. They decided not to return to their classes until the county's Board of Supervisors signed a statement to upgrade their inadequate schools. Although the protest was organized and carried out entirely by the students, the superintendent and school board members accused the school principal and other officials of orchestrating their pupils' actions. The strike and the consequent responses resulted in a request for help by Johns and the students from the National Association for the Advancement of Colored People (NAACP) legal office.

The protesting students attempted to meet with the school superintendent, T.J. McIlwaine, who refused the meeting. They proceeded to contact the chairman of the School Board Office, Maurice Large, who stated that he could not tell them when a new school would be built and advised them to return to school. Later, Johns and her committee sought the advice of a young minister, Reverend L. Francis Griffin, the pastor of the county's historical Black church. Griffin gave them the name of Spottswood Robinson III, representative of the NAACP legal office in Richmond, Virginia, who had won several cases in federal court to equalize teacher salaries and school facilities. Robinson received a letter signed by Carrie Stokes and Barbara Johns pleading for help and noting that the matter was of grave importance.

Robinson agreed to meet with the students; he drove with his partner, Oliver Hill, to Farmville to meet the strikers. Initially, the lawyer informed the students that they were not in compliance with the school attendance law and could be placed custody; however, one protester replied, "The jail was not big enough for all of us." Robinson, in awe of the students, resolved that he "would be interested in nothing short of a desegregation suit" (Irons 85).

The lawyers needed to gain the full support of the Black parents; they were going to attack segregated education instead of inequality at large. The students received overwhelming support from their parents by way of their signatures on a lawsuit seeking the end of separate schools in

Prince Edward County. Robinson and Hill filed the lawsuit, *Davis v. Prince Edward County* in the Richmond District Court on May 23, 1951. The first claimant was Dorothy Davis, a fifteen-year-old from Moton. The trial for the case occurred on Feb 25, 1952, and per Reverend Griffin's request, the courtroom was packed with parents from Prince Edward County who hoped that the five-day trial would settle. The lawyers, however, didn't share their optimism.

Nevertheless, volumes of evidence, verbal testimonies, and pictures displayed the inadequate condition and structure of the school facilities. The comparison between the White and Black schools was proven unequal in every respect. However, the three-judge panel, Dobie, Hutcheson, and Bryan, upheld segregation in Virginia and concluded that "indisputably," segregation "rests neither upon prejudice, nor caprice, nor any other measureless foundation." Instead, they claimed that it was just "one of the ways of life in Virginia." They found "no hurt or harm to either race" (Davis).

The judicial panel agreed that the facilities and curriculum at Moton High School were deficient and ordered the county "to pursue with diligence..." the correction of inequalities between the Black and White schools, but they upheld segregated schools. However, no timeframe or compliance reports were processed with the judges' decision (Davis). In response, the NAACP lawyers filed an appeal with the Supreme Court, joining the four others school desegregation cases in *Brown v. Board of Education of Topeka* in declaring that segregation in schools was unconstitutional.

The United States ruled on May 17, 1954, that racial segregation was against the law. The resulting battle between Virginia government officials was furious and lengthy. Within a few months of the 1954 decision, the governing body of Prince Edward County passed a resolution opposing desegregation and fully intending to resist the court order with all their might. They sent the resolution to all state officials. Additionally, the governor of Virginia appointed a thirty-two-member panel known as the "Gray's Commission" who were tasked with keeping the races separate within schools. The state and the county were working with the same agenda: to keep the schools segregated. To wit, laws of "massive resistance" (Virginia State Government) were incorporated, creating a united front of White politicians and leaders who were all intent on defying the *Brown* decision.

Senator Harry F. Byrd, Sr., a staunch segregationist, strongly supported "massive resistance" by promoting the "Southern Manifesto," a document signed by more than a hundred legislators from the South in 1956 who opposed integrated schools. The policy vehemently opposed the *Brown* decision and stated that it was "clear abuse of judicial power" (U.S. Supreme Court). He further argued that the federal government couldn't force the states to desegregate.

The Massive Resistance Laws that were passed in 1958 to prevent integration of schools, which incorporated the Pupil Placement Boards, tuition grants, and state funds. The Pupil Placement Boards were formed to assign specific students to particular schools, the tuition grants were provided to students who opposed integrated schools, and state funds were discontinued, closing any public school that agreed to integrate. Several schools in other districts adhered to the court order to integrate, such as Warren County, Charlottesville, and Norfolk, but they were blocked and closed in compliance with the school-closing law. In January 1959, the Virginia Supreme Court of Appeals reversed the school-closing law, and other counties reopened public schools on a desegregated basis when faced with the prospect of having no schools at all.

In June 1959, the Prince Edward County's Board of Supervisors rejected a school board budget for operating public schools during the 1959–1960 school years. In the fall of 1959, the public schools in Prince

Edward County were closed to all children, Black and White. There were "No Trespassing" signs on school property. The schools remained closed for five years (1959–1964). Because of the county's continued refusal to reopen the schools after the *Brown* decision was handed down, another case, *Griffin v. County School Board of Prince Edward*, was appealed to the U.S. Supreme Court in May 1964.

That case went before the United States Supreme Court as a result of resistance by the Prince Edward County Board of Supervisors. The Supreme Court decided that "the time for mere 'deliberate speed' has run out, and that phrase can no longer justify denying these Prince Edward County school children their constitutional rights to an education equal to that afforded by the public schools in the other parts of Virginia" (U.S. Supreme Court). The Griffin decision resulted in an order by the Supreme Court that demanded that Prince Edward County open its schools because the county violated the Equal Protection Clause of the 14th Amendment. However, the Prince Edward County Board of Supervisors met secretly to appropriate funds for private school education supported by tuition grants from state and tax credits from the county. The courts had forbidden such grants after the 1960–1961 school year, based on the argument that the state was participating in an unconstitutional attempt to evade the *Brown* decision. Eventually, all state and local efforts to resist integration collapsed, and the fight for integration in Prince Edward County ended in 1964 along with the massive resistance era in Virginia.

The only school district in the country that resorted to closing public school to avoid integration was Prince Edward County. On March 18, 1963, at the Kentucky Centennial of the Emancipation Proclamation, Robert F. Kennedy stated: "We may observe with much sadness and irony that, outside of Africa, south of the Sahara, where education is still a difficult challenge, the only places on Earth known not to provide free public education are Communist China, North Viet Nam, Sarawak, Singapore, British Honduras, and Prince Edward County, Virginia."

The student strike foreshadowed the coming of the civil rights movement. The United States has a long history of singling out groups of citizens, usually during war times, for special treatment under the law. It is not a new practice but invariably ends up being a tragic mistake. The events that took place in Prince Edward County after the courageous move by the students was tragic; people with political power rallied against rulings that would provide children the right to an education, just because of the color of their skin.

IX. MY ADULT LIFE

In September of 1967, following my traumatic high school years, I left home to attend Cortez Peters Business College in Washington, D.C. Mama took out loans to pay my tuition. The gentleman who taught me to type was the world's fastest typist on the manual typewriter. He had made appearances at many different events and even appeared on "The Ed Sullivan Show." To this day, I believe that technology slows a typist down in speed and accuracy. On the manual typewriter you had to be perfect; on the computer, you can delete and go back.

After my first year in business school, I entered the workforce, in job environments ranging from high school cafeterias to law offices. My most notable position during my early work years was a part-time clerical job I had under Attorney Dovey J. Roundtree, who is now retired. She was a leading civil rights lawyer, an Army veteran, and an ordained minister. She served for thirty-five years as general counsel to the National Council of Negro Women and as a special consultant of legal affairs to the African Methodist Episcopal Church. Mrs. Roundtree was a powerful force in the legal community and received numerous awards and honors for her achievements.

She attended Howard University Law School on the GI Bill and went on to break legal ground in both civil and criminal law. Upon her discharge from the military at the end of World War II, Mrs. Roundtree was looking for a way to make a difference, which led her to research cases for the legal team headed by Thurgood Marshall for what would become *Brown v. Board of Education*. She was the first Black woman admitted to the Bar Association of the District of Columbia and actively recruited other Black women attorneys. Mrs. Roundtree was considered one of the premier trial attorneys in the District of Columbia.

The end of my part-time position with her led me to several positions in federal service, the first of which was a GS-2 clerk typist position at the Department of the Navy, which I began in December of 1968. I worked during the day and attended classes at night. I graduated business school in June of 1969.

I got married in 1971, and in March 1973 I gave birth to a girl we named Erika Francine. I briefly left my full-time job with the federal government after she was born. I worked part-time for a Trademark Attorney from 10:00 a.m. to 2:00 p.m., which gave me more time in the mornings and afternoons to be with our baby. However, not long after I became a part-time worker, Earl got orders to go overseas to London, England. Before going overseas, we drove to Houston, Texas, to visit Earl's family. He got an opportunity to visit his father, but sadly, he passed away while we were overseas.

While in Middlesex, England, I resumed working for the United States government, and in August 1975, I gave birth to a second girl we named Robyn Arlean. In addition to having a second child, I returned to a military hospital for a hysterectomy in December 1975 and gallbladder surgery in December 1976. We returned to the States in 1977 and were met in New York by family and had a wonderful celebration. Earl was stationed in Washington, D.C., and I returned to work with the federal government. We moved into naval housing and later bought a house in Dale City, Virginia.

My federal employment lasted for more than thirty-six years, with positions ranging from clerical jobs to managerial and specialist positions in the human resources field. I was afforded many opportunities that included but were not limited to supervising, training, and traveling to various locations stateside and abroad. I retired from federal service in January 2006.

I returned to Prospect in September 2006.

*

It has always been difficult for me to talk about the closing of the schools and the impact that era has had on my life. After more than forty years, I began to open up and talk about that period in my life. I am indebted to my granddaughter, Mykhayla, for helping me get to the point where I could discuss it. Mykhayla used to ask me about events from the 1960s, and I shared my experiences with her. For example, I would arrive home from work after a rough day and she would greet me with "Hi, Grandma, what did you do at work today?" She continued with several more questions and waited patiently for my response.

X. NO LONGER SILENT

Today, years later, many memories of that period are still lost, but I know that a higher power is moving the silence away, and words are taking its place, bit by bit.

I have come to a place in my life where my voice is no longer silent. I feel a need to speak. I'm not always sure what I should be talking about, but I am certain that silence is no longer acceptable for me. I liken my forty years of silence to the calm after a severe summer storm: A gentle breeze does not disturb the leaves on the trees; the brightness of the sun's rays illuminates a rainbow among the clouds, which has no beginning or end.

Remaining silent—without a voice to express feelings and thoughts—caused me immense anguish. To internalize it again would be heartbreaking, and so instead, I have chosen to break that silence. I feel apprehensive and excited, an effect I attribute to three causes: a lack of knowledge, a lack of self-worth, and the recognition that I have achieved through counseling.

The teacher who announced that the schools would close in September of 1959 activated my years of silence. The instructor did not explain the school closing, and nobody else did, either. I did not understand why it was happening. I was taught that silence is golden—that if I sat there, listened, and waited, whatever life had in store for me would be revealed. Therefore, silence was my only defense. The lack of information I received from my mother caused even more turmoil and a sense of low self-worth.

Through counseling, I began to recognize that it was OK to speak about what I felt. The counselor told me that the continuous buildup of pain and hurt causes depression and poor health. I related self-worth to being good enough to attend school, get an education, and get a good job. I was convinced that I wasn't worthy enough to keep the schools open; it was tragic and destroyed my self-esteem. The despicable shame I felt would not subside because I couldn't talk about it. This was contrary to my personal belief that I controlled my own destiny. Fortunately, my counselor helped me to get in touch with my inner strengths and chart a course to use my strength to break the silence. I felt torn between my prior comfort zone of silence and the responsibility I felt to verbalize my thoughts.

Throughout it all, I had become complacent in my life of silence. As I began to realize this, the challenge of speaking up started causing me anxiety. My spirit was gradually awoken as I accrued better data, worked on enhancing my sense of self-worth, and got some superior, professional mental health guidance. I did a personal analysis of my progress and realized that it was acceptable for me to feel proud of my accomplishments.

*

My dream is to give voice to the victims who have not found their voices because the hurt and pain are too great. I want to break the silence so that the healing will begin for all of us. Poet and essayist Audre Lorde tells us "not to respect our fears more than we respect our needs to verbalize feelings; while we are silent, waiting to be free of fear, we will choke on the weight of that silence." I have come to believe that what is most important to me must be spoken—must be made verbal and shared—even at the risk of having it bruised or misunderstood.

XI. COMING TO A CROSSROAD

This section is dedicated to a special lady who made a difference in my life. I was forty years old, and she introduced me to two words that didn't have any meaning for me before our conversations: "self-esteem" and "dysfunctional." I don't know what course I will take from here, but I do know that I will always reflect back on the positive force of this individual. When I met her, I didn't know what I wanted, and I didn't have any plans to see her more than two or three times because I didn't want any help. I was "happy" being a victim, but I was wrong.

*

From time to time in life, we reach a point at which we need to turn around and make a change. We do not know for sure what the problem is, but we know that we need to do something differently. This portion of the book will address my process of trying to find out who I am, and why I am the way I am. I sought some assistance from a professional therapist and was given a task to write and reflect on different circumstances about myself and my family. Written below is what my belief system told me, as well as what I learned about myself and others through this process.

In life, we all have a beginning—birth—and an ending—death. Once I became an adult, when anyone asked me about my childhood, my very real and immediate reply was that I don't remember much about it.

I remembered that I wasn't taught how to show emotions such as love, sadness, or anger. I wasn't supposed to cry, laugh, or play too often, and I never expressed anger on a feeling level. I often recall a poem that I read by Angie Marie Flores from *Inspiration Poems* called "In Life":

In life there are people that will hurt us and cause us pain,

but we must learn to forgive and forget and not hold grudges.
In life there are mistakes we will make,
but we must learn from our wrongs and grow from them.
In life there are regrets we will have to live with,
but we must learn to leave the past behind and realize it is
something we can't change.
In life there are people we will lose forever and can't have back,
but we must learn to let go & move on.
In life there are going to be obstacles that will cause interference,
but we must learn to overcome these challenges and grow stronger.
In life there are fears that will hold us back from what we want,
but we must learn to fight them with the courage from within.
God holds our lives in his hands. He holds the key to our future.
Only He knows our fate.
He sees everything and knows everything.
Everything in life really does happen for a reason: "God's Reason."

I don't want to confuse *learning to love* with *being loved*. I felt that my mom loved me, but she never expressed that love in an emotional, caring way. I can't ever remember her hugging, kissing, or saying the words "I love you." Simple as they may seem, they are three of the hardest words in the English language for me to say. In later years, I learned to say "I love you," but it was not without great difficulty. I certainly mean it when I say these words and in no way take them lightly. Even to this day, I struggle with an expression of any kind. My feelings and responses are often intense and sometimes cause physical pain. In particular, anger is a repressed emotion for me. I don't know what it's like to express anger; it can be so intense that I feel like I might explode, but I won't allow it to come out. I sometimes misdirect my anger toward my girls, but I am more conscious of that these days.

The phrase "to thy self be true" is so critical to my well-being. To love me—feel good about myself—these are very easy words to say, but they are ever so difficult to accomplish. However, I have made some progress in this area. For brief periods of time, I do feel good about myself, but these feelings are typically short-lived. I've done a lot of thinking in this area, but with each setback, it becomes harder to return to my early memories. I often wonder why, and I would like to take this time to go back and rethink some issues that I feel may shed a little light on this area. I know I'll get stuck in some painful areas that I won't be able to recall fully, but I feel as if going forward depends on remembering.

*

I grew up in a household with my mom, grandma, two brothers, and an older sister and brother who left home when I was young. When I was about seven or eight years old, my grandmother had a stroke and became paralyzed, and I remember trying to take care of her by getting her food and helping her get outside and enjoy the nice weather. What stands out most in my mind is her telling me that I didn't fix her eggs right; she liked soft scrambled eggs. I remember being very careful and trying very hard to prepare them the way she liked them, but I guess she couldn't eat them because they were too hard.

More importantly, she would say that when I got old and couldn't do anything for myself, someone would treat me the same way as I treated her. What I heard was that I couldn't do anything right and would suffer for it when I grew up. I thought that I was very good and kind to her, of course. I never talked back and tried to do everything that she asked me to, but it was never good enough. Grandma died in her rocking chair holding my cousin's hand, and now that I think back on her death I was a non-entity; I couldn't even fix the damn eggs right. I couldn't even tell her that I was doing the best I could.

Why is this making me cry? Why am I holding back from really crying? What's going on that's causing me this pain? I should know the answers.

*

My mother worked very hard. She had jobs outside of the home doing housework, cooking, and catering parties. She took in ironing, did farming, and took care of her mother and children. My mother took care of sick in-laws, friends, and animals. I guess she did a little bit of everything. We had a horse, cows, hogs, chickens, dogs, and cats, and she loved everyone and would worry and become upset if anything happened to any of them.

Our mornings always started very early on the farm because there was always a lot to do before everyone went to work or school. The cows had to be fed, milked, and tied out; the horse, hogs, dogs, cats, and chickens had to be fed; and each of us had to have something to eat before leaving home. Somehow, I never felt hungry in the morning and didn't eat much, but there wasn't enough time for me to eat anyway.

I guess I'm jumping ahead a little. Before my grandmother's death, my mom stayed at home while we were in school, and during the summer months, she worked outside of the home because we were home to take care of Grandma. Grandma wasn't paralyzed during a portion of the time and didn't need anyone to stay with her.

I can't recall ever doing anything that made Mother happy, either: The biscuits wouldn't turn out right; I shouldn't have poured the water out of the potatoes because we didn't have fresh milk to make mashed potatoes; I forgot to sweep the dirt. What I didn't do always got noticed. However, I was a generally a very good child and didn't give her a moment of trouble. We didn't talk about anything too much, and I was always quiet. Of course, I never could talk back or be angry about anything because she would tell me that I was getting "too grown" or "too smart," and that was cause for punishment. Therefore, I didn't get punished. I didn't even ask questions about any school homework but just did the best I could.

*

I'm going to return to the present at this point. I think to myself, so what if I don't care about myself when I'm not hurting anyone except myself? I now realize how wrong I am. I can see in my daughters the product of my self-worth. I recognize how my repressed emotions affected their upbringing. I reflect back on the positive forces of my therapist, and I hear questions such as, "How will they know that it's OK to cry when you hide your tears from them? How will they learn to comfort you when you don't allow them to comfort you? How will they learn to be compassionate when you show them no compassion?" She encouraged me with statements like, "Don't shield them from pain and hurt, for it's a part of life. Be happy with who and what they are."

Living in a household that emits negative forces brews inner turmoil and low self-worth. "Self-esteem" was a foreign word to me until about two years ago, and I wonder how many people live and die not knowing that such a word exists. It's sad that some people never learn to appreciate the gift that is life: You survive, you exist, and you go on until the end. What happens in between creates another word that's buried somewhere in the subconscious: "choice." It's up to me, after a certain age, to choose what course my life will take. Oh, how I struggle to communicate what I feel. I've come a long way from where I used to be, and I work every day to be what I want to be. I don't know what's holding me back. I do know that I want to release my feelings, needs, and desires, but I always stop before reaching the scream. Why?

*

I'll go back to my memories of childhood now and talk a little more about my mom, who I dearly loved. I know that she loved me and gave me the best that she had to give. However, thinking back, I realize that she didn't know how to show and tell about that love. It just wasn't a part of her makeup. Her way was to criticize and put down; nothing I did was right or good enough. I can remember rushing home from school and trying to get all my chores done before Mom came home so that she would say, "That's good," or "You did a good job," but she never did. Instead, she asked me, "Why didn't you take your school clothes off?" or "Did you get the cow?" or she would point out something that I had accidentally left undone. She said, "I work so hard, and I'd think you children would want to do something to help out around here." I thought I had. I can also remember very briefly trying to explain why something didn't get done or why something happened only to be told to be quiet or shut up. I learned how to be quiet and not say anything; if I did, I was accepted because I didn't cause any problems. I would overhear my mother saying when she was talking to someone else: "I can't get Al to say anything, she is so quiet."

These days, I can more vividly recall some parts of my childhood that I have not remembered before, and in some respects, I understand some things a little better now. I feel like I have dealt with most of the issues as far as my mother is concerned, but even though she's no longer with me, I feel like I haven't let go of enough to move on truly. I don't know whether I am unable to deal with the loss or that I do not recall something that may have happened when she was alive. I realize that she did her best, but I can't seem to express some of the thoughts that go through my mind, not even in writing them down. I can think about what I should have said when I felt pain, sadness, or fear, but I can't say the words out loud. I can't even talk out loud to myself.

*

My dad didn't live with us. He lived in Baltimore with one of my mother's brothers and his family. My dad would come home on some holidays and weekends, and I can remember always being glad to see him because he saw me as a person and would talk to me. He always wanted to know how I was doing and what I was doing. We would spend time together cooking and going places. However, I can't ever remember saying goodbye to him when he left. I visited him a few times one summer, and we always had a good time. I never told my father that I loved him. I guess I wish that I had more time with him, but that wasn't in God's plan. Nevertheless, in our short relationship, my memories are good.

XII. MY AUNTS

My aunts were also instrumental during my childhood. Aunt Estelle was a very quiet lady who took her time and rarely showed any anger. She was a very hard worker, and she hid her illness from other family members. She suffered from high blood pressure and often had angina, which she tried to hide from all of us. For example, she always had her nitroglycerin tablets with her, and on occasions when walking, she would need to stop and put a tablet under her tongue.

I don't remember her playing an active role in my life until the schools closed. After the school closures, we stayed with my uncle, brother to Aunt Estelle and my mom, and his family in the same house that my father lived in before his death. I shared a room with Aunt Estelle for the three years while we attended school there. They treated me similarly to how my mother did, and I responded similarly in turn. I remember going to school and needing lunch money or other things, but being afraid to ask for them if Aunt Estelle forgot to give them to me. At some point, she would find out or remember and scold me for not asking. The next time I needed something, I would finally ask after worrying about the consequences of not having what I needed.

One day that stands out very vividly is the day I was on my period and messed up my dress and had to walk home trying to hide the stain. After I got home, I washed and cleaned everything and gathered up enough courage to tell my aunt I needed more sanitary pads. The ironic thing about that whole incident is that the accident happened because I couldn't bring myself to ask permission to go to the bathroom during class. I seemed to have trouble asking for what I needed, and I guess that's because I felt as if I would cause problems for someone else. All of the women in my family seemed to deal with similar anxieties. Aunt Estelle worried a great deal about her sisters' illnesses but neglected her well-being. She tried to take care of my mother, which caused my mother to worry about her while playing down her discomfort.

One of my last memories of Aunt Estelle was after my mother died. I was taking her home after she visited her youngest sister who was extremely ill in the hospital. Even though she was very quiet, I saw the pain in her eyes and heard the sadness in her voice. I sensed tiredness in her that was unnerving; it was as if she was saying in her quiet, unassuming manner, "I have fought the good fight, I have run the race, and I am ready to go home forever." I even commented to my sister later about the way our aunt seemed and how hard she was taking Aunt Minnie's illness and imminent death.

Aunt Estelle passed quietly away within a week of that ride home. After visiting Aunt Minnie in the hospital and taking Aunt Estelle to her house, I returned to my home in Dale City. The following night church service was being held in Prospect, and friends and neighbors felt that Aunt Estelle should stay home and rest instead of attending church. However, she insisted that she wanted to attend church services. I believe she knew that it would be her last time, perhaps through a dream or the grief of losing one sister and the other sister terminally ill. She spoke about her desire of not wanting to live without her sisters on the ride to her house from the hospital. Later we learned from her grandson that she had spoken to him about the arrangements for her home-going service.

*

Sometimes, life situations can rock your world. In 1990, I became a volunteer with Action through Community Service (ACTS). I completed the course of training via ACTS Turning Points in navigating domestic violence, and I volunteered at the shelter a few nights a week. There are two poems that I received during that training that will always be a part of my memory, one called "Remember" and the other called "Just Listen." These poems remind us about our responsibilities.

On Thursday evening, when I arrived home around 11:00 p.m. from the shelter, my girls were still awake and on the phone. They handed it to me and told me that their dad wanted to talk to me. After trying to prepare myself for the news that my Aunt Minnie, who was in the hospital, had passed, I took the phone.

Earl said he had some bad news.

I waited a moment and said, "Aunt Minnie is gone."

He replied, "No, sit down."

I felt frightened and could not imagine what happened, and then he told me it was Aunt Estelle. I remember sitting down, getting up, moving about, crying, and only allowing my girls to comfort me a little. I refused Earl's offer to come over. I went through the motions of getting ready to leave because it was automatic; I had played that role so many times before.

I had become accustomed to tiredness. I had been exhausted in the past few weeks from going back and forth to be with Aunt Minnie, trying to work, volunteering at the shelter, and taking care of the girls. The exhaustion suddenly didn't belong to me anymore. It had temporarily left my body. I often wonder how many people go through life never knowing that you can share feelings and make decisions about your own life. Who can that hurt? Until lately, I would answer that question with "no one."

*

My other aunt and her husband were also fundamental to my childhood years. Aunt Minnie always seemed to be unhappy or upset, especially if a family member did not seem to pay any attention to her in some way. Her actions seemed to make people want to stay away from her; they said that her bark was a lot worse than her bite. She wanted attention, and when she felt she was not getting it, she became hurt and upset and would lash out at others with hurtful words. She appeared to be an unhappy lady who sought acceptance and comfort from men and fought to make anyone like her.

In actuality, I guess she never really cared a great deal about herself. All she wanted was for others to say, "Minnie did a good job" or "Minnie made what she did in life worthwhile." Her family loved and cared for her and protected her to the limits she would allow and to the limits they could express. When I was a child, I wondered why she was unhappy and what *I* had done to cause her to be so bitter.

I now realize that it was not my fault. Auntie lived and died without knowing that the only person she needed to satisfy was herself and that happiness was a gift that only she could give herself. I was around her when I was needed for work, but again and again, my efforts proved to be unsatisfactory. I kept doing whatever was needed to the best of my ability.

*

An uncle abused me during my pre-teen years. I now recognize it as a major trauma in my life. To be kissed and fondled when I was eleven and twelve years old was a very frightening experience. At the time, I felt very uncomfortable and knew that it wasn't right, but my uncle told me not to tell anyone, especially my mother or aunt because they would be very angry at me.

This abuse occurred every time I was alone with him for about a year and a half. I remember when it stopped. I was asthmatic as a child, and one day during the summer, I was at home alone, and he came to visit. I backed away from him and became very scared, and I started to have a very bad asthma attack. I was gasping for breath, and he thought that I would not recover and left me alone. He never tried anything after that day.

Once I was able to speak about the abuse, I told my sister, who is eleven years older than I am. She shared with me that he had done the same thing to her when she was around the same age as I was at the time. I often wonder how many other girls had to experience his abuse because of they were afraid to tell anyone. I believe that we weren't the only two.

*

I could talk about each member of my family endlessly, but the strange thing about it is that I can see and feel a part of each of them in me. For as long as I can remember, I have known some of their inner thoughts and turmoil—some from my observation and others from them telling me. On more than a few occasions, they would confide in me about how they felt. I could feel and hear the pain, but I never felt unpretentious happiness. Don't get me wrong, there have been happy times, but everyone plays a part in not allowing their real thoughts or feelings to show through.

Among my family members, I have discovered one commonality: In each, certain needs are not met, which prevented them from being able to validate their feelings of self-worth. I don't want to give the impression that I'm in any way trying to blame anyone or find fault in the way people are. In so many cases, you don't know what you don't know.

I recall reading in "Breaking the Silence" that when people ask how we're doing, we usually respond with a perfunctory, "Fine, just fine," no matter how depressed or off-center we may feel. Although there are a lot of good reasons not to invite co-workers, neighbors, and casual acquaintances into our emotional worlds, often we hide our pain from family and close friends who care deeply about our well-being.

For a long time, I was in deep emotional pain, crying when I could be alone. Sometimes to breathe was painful, but each day when I went out, I would bury that pain somewhere and pretend that everything was "just fine." I would hide from everyone who was close to me: my great anxiety when money was short, when relationships weren't working, or when there was trouble on the job. For a long time, I wouldn't speak honestly about my hurt and fears because admitting them meant I was having difficulty coping, and that some part of my life was a failure. I was silent because I didn't want to burden people. But not being able to speak about my feelings reflected my inability to fully examine my life, because denying our truths to others makes us deny them to ourselves.

XIII. MY DAUGHTERS

Erika

Now it is time for me to write about the people who are closest to my heart and most dear to me: Erika, your mother, Robyn, your aunt, and you. Erika was born in the Bethesda Naval Hospital in Maryland on March 12, 1973. Your grandfather, Earl, witnessed her birth, and like you, she was a beautiful baby who grew into a beautiful woman.

My portion of this story will focus on her upbringing, and that was interesting at best. She was a very curious, inquisitive little girl. Erika would want to know the "who, what, when, where, and why" of everything. Once she learned to talk, her dad and I spent a lot of time answering questions and explaining little things to her. For example, as a pre-teenager, she was very anxious to wear makeup and needed to know the precise time and date she would be allowed to do so. Erika was involved in quite a few activities growing up, such as the Brownies and then the Girl Scouts. She played the viola in school, which took us to many different places for concerts. As she grew up, we went through sleepovers, wearing makeup, driving, dating, and becoming who she is today. However, the best way for me to honor her is to let her tell you her own stories and memories through her "blogs" and "writings."

Erika's Blogs

5-22-2013

So, my mom asked me to begin writing my memories. She asked Robyn, too. She says she wants to add them to her memoirs. I think this is a great project, and in writing, I will probably remind myself and others of things that have happened over my forty years. My memory is pretty darned good if I do say so myself!

Where to begin, where to begin? I won't begin at the beginning; I don't remember being in the womb. I think my mind is a series of thoughts, snippets, mini-movies, and run-on sentences. I'm truly hoping that you will find this helpful, Mom.

Until I was four, we lived in London, England. Dad was in the Navy, so we traveled. I think London is the only place my mom went with my dad. Once we headed back to the States (Granby Road in Dale City, Virginia), Mom said that she wasn't traveling anymore with the military and that she wanted to raise the kids in one place. So, I was a year old when we went to London. My sister, Robyn, was born in London, so technically, she could've had dual citizenship. But, I digress...

I don't know if these are memories or just things that I know about our time in London and a few years after. I was the only one who developed an English accent. What can I say? Those were my formative years! I guess I said things like "rubbish" and "bloody."

We had a nanny named Lynn. I wonder if Mom still keeps in touch with her. I know that my kindergarten teacher found it strange that I had an accent and waited with me on the curb in front of the school for my dad to pick me up. I'm assuming she wanted to know if he had an accent too. I remember Dad telling me that he put me on the phone with Aunt Willie, and I babbled on like any four- or five-year-old would. When I handed the phone back to Dad, Aunt Willie promptly told him that no one in our family sounded like that and to put her niece on the phone! HA! In Prospect the elders sat me on a stool in the middle of the kitchen and asked me questions so they could hear the accent. I, completely oblivious, indulged them.

I was a chatty little girl until I realized that I didn't sound like anyone else. My chatter was glaringly obvious in middle school. The other black kids didn't like me because I sounded too "proper" and they thought I was a "wannabe." I was called a "cracker." Of course, I didn't understand right away. I mean, what was the big deal?! I spoke English just like they did. Or did I? Needless to say, I kept my head down and was quiet for the most part. Don't get me wrong; I had some great friends, and I enjoyed middle school. It's just that middle school was when I found out that some differences are *too* different for some people to handle.

High school was better. I still didn't talk a whole lot except to my friends. I guess you could say I was popular. Other black students started to accept me even though I was still "different." I had real hair that was long! That was different! And once you learn to speak a certain way, you don't lose it, so I was still labeled "proper." I loved high school, though. I think I found a lot of my voice in high school.

*

5-23-2013

I love morning conversations with my mom! I typically call her on the way to work two or three times per week. Then, there's the Saturday on-my-way-home-from-the-gym call. We gab about day-to-day stuff. She gives me advice. She listens to me. So, this morning, we were talking about the writing and how neat it would be to publish our collaborative efforts. I already know a lot of people who would be interested in reading our book.

When Robyn and I were young and living on Granby Road, we used to listen to music and dance all the time. We listened to our parents' albums—Four Tops, Temptations, Natalie Cole, Aretha Franklin, Supremes, Marvin Gaye, and much more. We had a blast, just the two of us, listening to music and dancing. "Disco Inferno" was one of our favorites. "Papa Was a Rolling Stone" was a good one too.

Mom and Dad loved music! Dad used to sing, and one of his absolute favorite's songs was "Duke of Earl." Of course! You know he thought that song was written for him! I also remember my grandmother and uncles on our mother's side listening to music. Music was always a part of our upbringing and always part of almost any gathering.

As Robyn and I got older, music remained a big part of our lives. We used to watch MTV *a lot*. Anita Baker has this song called "Sweet Love," and there was a video to go with it. Anita had this weird dance that she did in the video where she shrugged her shoulders up and rocked from side to side. Robyn did this dance perfectly! I'm not even lying! We used to laugh hysterically every time she or Anita did it. Not too long ago, I asked Mykhayla to ask her aunt to do the dance next time she saw her, and Robyn said, "Absolutely not."

So, our love of music remains. I've passed that love onto my daughter, Mykhayla. I have taught her since she was little that all music comes from other music. The samples that current musicians use come from older songs. I quiz that girl to this day! I needed her to understand that music is a journey, and I am still teaching her. Heck, I'm still learning!

Mykhayla is very talented. She sings beautifully, plays the piano, and is teaching herself the guitar. I'm glad her love of music comes from a place of family and love.

*

5-28-2013

Having a biracial child has been somewhat interesting. Mykhayla was a very fun baby and child. She made me laugh and still makes me laugh!

Anyway, back to the biracial thing. Mykhayla was VERY pale when she was born. Almost translucent. That made for a few interesting observations. The receptionist at my OB's office even asked me if Mykhayla was my baby. Really? When I said yes, she said, "But she's so…so…FAIR!" You think?! It's not like she hadn't seen Mykhayla's biological dad.

One of my favorite moments with race was when Stephanie (one of Mykhayla's godmothers), Mykhayla, and I went to BJ's Wholesale Club. A Caucasian woman came up to us and looked at Mykhayla, looked at me, looked at Mykhayla, looked at Stephanie, then turned toward ME, and said, "What a beautiful baby!" I wanted to hug her!

Stephanie and Mykhayla looked alike at the time. She has curly brown hair and fair skin. But Mykhayla's features looked like mine. Most strangers who I ran into just judged our relationship by skin color and not features. Now that Mykhayla has gotten older, she and I truly look alike except for skin color. Someone once told me that it looked like I spit her out. Sounds gross, but I get what they were saying!

When Mykhayla was about three, Mom and I were watching a made-for-TV movie about Sojourner Truth. Mykhayla was riding her little tricycle around the house. She made it back into the room where the TV was, looked at the TV, and asked if we were watching a movie about "you guys." As you can imagine, the silence was deafening. Mom looked at Mykhayla and then looked at me. I looked at Mykhayla, then at Mom. I told Mykhayla that I was her mother, and mom was her grandmother so that this movie was about her too! She just said OK and moved on. She saw color but probably didn't understand that it was anything more than color.

7-23-2013

Leftover Magic

My sister, Robyn, wrote an entry about food. I realized that food was and still is very important to our family. I posted something about "leftover magic" on my Facebook page not too long ago. My mom has that skill where she can pull random bits of leftovers out of the fridge and make a gourmet meal! Y'all think I'm playing, but I'm not. GOURMET, I tell you!

Anyway, I finally got some of the leftover magic myself. I had a little bit of leftover steak, some scalloped potatoes, and some onion. You don't even know how good this meal was. And I prepared it out of some leftovers.

Mom makes the BEST potato pancakes out of leftover mashed potatoes. I still get mad because mine don't turn out like hers do. She also does this wingette in the microwave thing. Not leftovers per se, but magic. Let me cook some wingettes in the microwave... they would never turn out like my mom's. It's like there is a special gene that moms have that doesn't get passed down. Although, I think Mykhayla has the leftover magic gene. Dang.

*

8-27-2013

Many of my childhood memories involve food. Whether it was learning to cook or eating a dish that "only my mom could make," food was a big part of our upbringing. I honestly don't remember *how* I learned to cook, only that I learned to cook. We watched my mom cook a lot. I believe she used to tell us that if you could read, you could cook. My mom is an amazing baker, so she was big into recipes. I did not get the great baker gene.

Grandma Flossie also let us watch and help her cook. We got little jobs like pouring ingredients into a mixing bowl and getting ingredients from the cabinet or refrigerator. Sometimes, she even let us (me mainly) chop or cut things. Grandma Flossie was very concerned with how we used knives.

When we were young, Mom made some of the best food. Gravy bread was a favorite. Mom would make a dish that involved gravy, and then she would take a regular slice of bread, pour gravy over it, and slice it into bite-sized squares. So simple, but *so* good! Robyn and I even tried it as adults to see if it was still good, and it was! We also used to eat Hamburger Helper like it was our job. It was easy and relatively good for us. Now we know that most packaged foods have way too much sodium, but that's neither here nor there. Hamburger Helper was an easy meal, perfect for a single mom to cook for her two young children. Mom usually opened a can of green beans to go with it.

Now, on the weekends, when Mom had more time to cook, you already know that she would throw down! Fried chicken, fried fish, macaroni and cheese, collard greens, homemade rolls, pinto beans, etc. I'm forty and still have trouble making my fried chicken taste like Mom's. I come close, though.

Grandma Flossie had her signature dishes, too. Spaghetti with a sauce made from scratch, smothered chicken (which I did not eat because I was super picky and highly opposed to the sauce), homemade rolls, rice pudding, bread pudding, banana pudding, etc. Grandma always had a pot of something on the stove when we arrived, no matter the time of day or night.

My dad was a great cook, too. He was more of an experimenter, though. I got to the point where if he wouldn't tell me what was in it, I wasn't eating it. He had this habit of slipping random organs into stuff. I know one time Dad made a curry dish, and Mom was mad about it! Mom rode in a vanpool with a gentleman who ALWAYS smelled of curry, and she couldn't deal with it. And then Dad cooked some curry in her house?! Nope. Uh-uh. That was not the move! We boiled cinnamon on the stove for a few days to get rid of the smell.

My daughter, Mykhayla, has learned to cook from all of us, I think. I know I gave her little jobs. I taught her how to use the microwave and that the stove could be dangerous. In fact, when I first started letting her use the stove on her own, I made her call me when she started cooking and again when she finished cooking. Have to make sure that flame is off!

I can't imagine NOT cooking and NOT sharing food with my friends and family. I know that I've learned from the best and continue to learn. I still call my mom or sister to help me out with something I want to cook or to retrieve or borrow a recipe.

*

4-19-2015

It's been a long time… I shouldn't have left you…

It's been eight months since I last posted. I had no idea it had been that long. I kind of feel like I'm starting over with blogging. At least I can always come back to it.

I owe this particular post to Andrea/Drieky. Her recent post motivated me, spoke to me, and frankly, made me a little teary. Thank you, Sweetie!

Anyway, it's been a long time. And what the heck do I write about?! I created this blog to share my fitness journey. Then, it morphed into more than that. In fact, I NEED it to be more than that. I'm not just going through a FITNESS journey. I'm going through a life journey. Fitness for me is going to be a lot more involved than I thought it would be.

I'm sure I've shared this before, but I have Hashimoto's (Hashi's) and polycystic ovarian syndrome. Both of these "things" can keep me from losing weight AND cause me to gain weight. CURSES!

Hashimoto's is an autoimmune disease, and there is no cure. Yes, it can go into remission, but there is no cure. Now, it can be managed by meds, diet, and natural remedies. I can't even remember how long ago I was diagnosed, but I DO know that I believed my first endo when he said, "Take this pill every day. You'll be on it for the rest of your life. You'll be fine."

I didn't feel fine, so I ditched Endo #1 and went to Endo #2. I'm still with #2, but I suspect I'll be moving onto another soon.

I messed up by taking #1's word. You know, he was a doctor. He was smarter than I was. He knew what he was talking about. Well, not really. The one thing he didn't know was ME. Every person who is diagnosed with Hashi's presents differently, and different treatments work for some and not for others.

Last year, I started to do some research. I'm finding out SO MUCH! It's intimidating, but I am determined to learn as much as possible and determine what makes *me* feel the best that I can. So, this is the tip of the iceberg. Expect to hear more. Blogging will help me because it's an easy way to keep a record and something I can refer to.

Thanks for reading!

*

6-18-2015

Don't worry... Don't PANIC!

So, I'm about to finish up my twelve-week autoimmune protocol (AIP) diet, and I'm still going strong! I've reintroduced two more items: red wine and chocolate. Red wine seems to be fine. I just don't have the urge to drink a whole lot of it. Not sure about chocolate. I may have to try that again when I haven't eaten a new cabbage dish for the two days prior.

Again, a bonus of AIP (for me anyway) is weight loss. I am constantly surprised by this. I've maintained or gained for so many years. LOSING weight is refreshing and startling all at the same time. I keep expecting to gain it back. I know I shouldn't, but I swear the years of maintaining and gaining have brainwashed me. I'm working on a revised way of thinking. I'm wearing things in my closet that I haven't worn in YEARS!

I haven't talked about working out so much lately. I still do it. I have a solid three workouts per week. Two Zumba classes and one tap class. Three days per week seems to work for me, although I plan to add some weight/strength training. That's something I can do at home in addition to the workouts I have outside of my home. Tap will end this weekend, so I'll have to add another cardio workout to maintain my three.

I'm still happy with AIP. I'll admit I can get a little down sometimes about what I can't eat, but I get over it rather quickly. Like I've said before, I've figured out how to make my comfort foods compliant. When I need them, I can make them!

I also feel good about educating others about AIP and Hashimoto's. They are not easy topics to discuss or easy to get people to understand. Hell, any autoimmune disease is tough to explain. I think bringing these diseases to the forefront can only help those of us who suffer from them. More collaboration, more discussion, more support! I know that I am very lucky to have supportive family and friends. I didn't talk about it at all when I was first diagnosed other than to say what my issue was. After a few years, I realized that the little pill wasn't working, so I started my research. After that, I realized I needed to talk about it more to make people understand that's it not just something that can be taken care of with a pill.

Rambling again!

I want you to realize that if you have an autoimmune disease, you're not alone. There is support out there if you're not getting support at home.

It's almost Friday, y'all! Have a great weekend.

Robyn

Now I will discuss my second and last child, Robyn. Robyn was born in Middlesex, England, on Aug 20, 1975. Having a child overseas was quite a different experience than having a child in the United States. Robyn was also a beautiful baby and grew into a lovely, striking adult. Robyn was very curious about everything too, but unlike Erika, she was more of an explorer and wanted to investigate things for herself. She wanted to touch and pick up insects, and this was a bit stressful for me if she encountered something that could potentially hurt her, such as a bee.

Robyn tried playing an instrument in school but was interested in being a part of the wrestling team as an assistant. We traveled to different schools for some of these events. Robyn also trained in the martial art Tae Kwon Do and received a green degree belt, but I'll have to check with her on the degree and color. She also attended a few competitions and had the honor of meeting Jhoon Rhee. Robyn was also editor-in-chief for her high school news magazine, and at some point, I believe she aspired to be a journalist. I will also honor Robyn by allowing her to tell her memories in her blogs and writings. Some of her writings were written for me and others for her school magazine, *The Hyphen*, as indicated below.

Robyn's Blogs

5-23-2013

Purpose

The purpose of this journal is to satisfy a request from my mother. She has written some memoirs for my niece and would like to include stories from my sister and me, so I guess I better write them. I think I would like to write about my coming-out story, the story about the 1-800 numbers, and the cell phone. I would like to highlight my mother's gentle, modest, humble, and meek nature. I would like to discuss how my mother helped to create the world that I live in today and how she has passed her legacy to me.

5-26-2013

Air Florida, Flight 90

In January of 1982, I was six years old, and we were on our third babysitter that I remember, Mrs. Teel. She was our sitter all the way through high school (why we went to a sitter all the way through high school is another story for another day).

As far back as I remember, my sister and I were roused at around 4:30 a.m. to go to a sitter because my mom worked in Washington, D.C. In 1982, I believe she was working at the Navy Yard. She rode in a commuter van at that time and drove to the commuter lot after dropping us off.

My mother worked for the federal government for nearly thirty-five years, and that means she commuted from Woodbridge, Virginia, to Washington, D.C., every day for thirty-five years to provide us all with the life we were accustomed to. I didn't understand the sacrifice until I was older, but now I get it.

My mom traveled daily up I-95, onto I-395 (also known as the Beltway), and across the 14th Street bridge, which goes into the city. As a six-year-old, I didn't comprehend all of my mother's daily routine, but some phrases that stood out to me about her daily life were "sitting on the 14th Street Bridge" and "stuck on the beltway." Those things were part of our standard, everyday conversations. She was often late picking us up from Mrs. Teel's house due to "sitting on the beltway" or "sitting on the 14th Street Bridge."

On one particular day in January, there was a pretty fierce snowstorm, and the federal government closed early, at around 3:00 p.m. I'm not sure if I knew that at the time, but I knew enough to know not to expect my mom early due to the weather. At some point, a newsperson came on the late afternoon show and stated that a Boeing 737 crashed into the 14th Street Bridge. Hours passed, and they began to show footage of the crash. There were people amongst the ice chunks going into shock in the Potomac River, and I quietly searched the screen for my mom. The newscasters didn't mention which side of the bridge was hit, and I didn't know enough to know that it is a five-lane bridge. Mrs. Teel kept a few other kids, and she had a daughter my age. We all were glued to the television, probably all looking for my mom in the water. I remember seeing a black lady in the water, and I scooted a little closer to the TV, but the hair was wrong; it wasn't her.

Hours passed, and my mom still didn't pick us up. We might have had dinner there, but I'm not sure. I remember being very quiet, and all of the others in the home were trying to be reassuring, but I just wanted them to stop. They weren't helping me feel any better. I was just a kid, and I thought if I could at least see my mom in the water, I would know where she was.

Of course, my mother had no idea that we were so worried. She recalls leaving work early, and a member of the vanpool wasn't there, so they had to wait. Then when they got to the bridge, traffic came to a dead stop. Traffic on the bridge was nothing new. Then, they looked over and saw a that the plane had hit the other side of the bridge. There were sirens and rescuers and helicopters, and the traffic wasn't moving. It didn't occur to her, however, that there was news footage and that people were worried. She arrived at the commuter lot tired, and a nice gentleman helped her clean the snow off of her car. The gentleman also had no way to get home, so she drove him.

When the doorbell rang at Mrs. Teel's house, I didn't want to get my hopes up that it was her, though I was hoping badly that it was. I was never so happy to see another person in my life. I don't remember much of the ride home, except that the drama wasn't quite over because we still had to make it home safely. I'm still not sure if my mom understands exactly how concerned I was sitting so close to the TV, looking for her in the water, knowing that she cannot swim and trying not to think the worst with my six-year-old brain.

6-23-2013

The Food

I guess you all are going to want to know about the food. I have to reiterate that my mom got us out of the house at 4:30 a.m. regularly and that we didn't get home until after 5:00 p.m. during the week. But while we were still little, she packed our lunches every day and cooked us a hot dinner every night. I suppose we ate breakfast at the sitter's house most days.

Parenting is different these days; everyone is hypersensitive about doing the best for their children, and I understand that, but my mom's best was plenty good enough. My favorite meal to eat in front of the TV in the evening was fried pork chops and Kraft macaroni and cheese (there were probably some green beans or something, but I'm telling the story).

To this day, my mother's spaghetti is the best kind of meal a person could eat. Every mother has a few specialty items, "signature dishes," if you will. My mother is the maker of homemade bread, potato salad, and fried chicken. Don't get me wrong, she cooks nearly everything well, but her "public frequently requests those." When we were kids, she was always cooking for some function—a luncheon at work or a holiday meal. We got sent to school with our delicious American cheese and Miracle Whip sandwiches, while mom was packing up homemade bread and fried chicken for her colleagues. How dare her! I'm just kidding; we did usually get to share in the spoils of the frequent work functions.

On the weekends and holidays, it wasn't unheard of for Mom to cook fresh greens: collards, creasy, and kale. We also ate pig feet, hog maws, chitterlings, and ribs. My father was known to get a bushel of live blue crabs occasionally, and we would spread out newspaper, invite the neighbors, and have a blast cooking and eating the crabs. Dad always had to have a sword fight with a live crab just before its demise, just for the show of it.

After we were old enough for our parents (mostly my mom) to sleep in later than we did, my older sister took on the responsibility of making us breakfast while we watched Sesame Street and Electric Company on Saturday mornings. Though I am certain her palate has matured, that sister of mine was SUCH a picky eater; it appeared that she preferred cooking more than she did eating. She would painstakingly make me perfectly creamy, no-lump Cream of Wheat (we were *gourmet*), while she ate ketchup sandwiches, which she loved. (I wouldn't be surprised if she still ate them to this day.)

When we got a little older, my sister learned how to make omelets. I think we got a second-hand omelet pan from a thrift store run with Dad. She loved to make omelets. She would put everything in the fridge in them. She would say, "I'm going to make you an omelet." It didn't matter what I was doing—sleeping, watching TV, whatever. If she felt like making an omelet, it was my responsibility to eat it (she didn't eat eggs). Eventually, my sister moved on to making quiche. My mother and sister have both added many things to their cooking repertoire that are staples in our households. I can cook, but I'd rather do something else. Besides, they *like* to cook.

One of our parents' friends from the Philippines taught us to make lumpia once, and we ran with it. It became our family's "signature item." Lumpia is required at every family function with our homemade sweet-and-sour sauce (we have to collaborate and taste to remember the recipe each time). When we were in high school, we talked about starting a catering business, which honestly probably could've succeeded if we had pursued it.

Food is always something that we have passed down in our family. Cooking and eating have always been a big part of what makes our family special. I remember showing up to my grandmother's house in the middle of the night, and she had a pot of beans on the stove and some fresh fried chicken for us to eat. Food is just what we do. Your Aunt Robyn wrote the following as a Christmas gift for me in 2004. It is a truly wonderful gift, and I believe her childhood dream of where she lives today. The sketch shows a picture of her and her grandma feeding the hogs.

*

You won't find it on any map, but if you follow these directions closely, you'll arrive, in no time, to the town of Prospect, Virginia. It's quite a small town, to my memory, just the post office and two small family stores. Bordered by railroad tracks that you have to remember to stop at, Prospect is an unsophisticated little village that remains untouched by big city buildings, the hustle and bustle, and in my memory will forever remain that way.

Just after Farmville, but a good distance from Lynchburg on Route 460 West, make a left onto Route 608. Don't forget to stop at the railroad crossing; there might be a train coming. Proceed down the winding road, making sure to wave at any folks sitting on their porches. It doesn't matter if you know them or not; it's just the cordial thing to do. Just around the bend, make a left at the White folks' church (no violation intended; that's just what it's called). Slow down to cross the one-car bridge (there's a weight limit). If another car is approaching, pull over and wait; it's just good manners.

Just after the hilltop where the Sunday school was held, and the hunting club had its shooting matches, among other things, you'll arrive at Mrs. Carter's house. Mrs. Carter's house, if you're in my family, is always the first and last stop you make during the visit to Prospect. Mrs. Carter was quite the pillar of the small community. She, as one of Prospect's oldest residents, knew virtually everything and everybody in and around town. She taught and babysat all the relatives who seemed old to me when I was young. She was active in the church as a secretary, and I can't remember a function she did not attend.

On down the road, pass Aunt Minnie's house. Just about everyone in town had hens, and a few people had ducks, but Aunt Minnie had pheasants. She also had a car. And what a car it was! It was so shiny and so green; it was almost surreal. Aunt Minnie was the official driver for the family when no one's grown children were visiting. The "green machine" always had a clean scent that reminded me of the church, probably because that's generally where we went in it. The smell was a mixture of Aunt Minnie's wig and peppermint candy. I'm not sure what a wig smells like really, but that's what the clean fragrance brought to mind. Aunt Minnie always had a banana or some other type of fruit that we kids just had to have. We usually stopped at Aunt Minnie's house on the way out of town also.

Back to the directions: After passing my Uncle Roy's house (it's got the blue truck), Ms. Fannie's, and the Allens', make a left at Ms. Rachel's store. To be honest, I have no idea who Ms. Rachel is, and I heard that the store burned down before I was born, but that's where you turn. At this point, slow down; this part is a little rockier than the rest. Besides, you may see a dog, cat, hen, duck family, or some other class of beast in the road. On a normal basis, there isn't too much traffic here, so the animals roam free. I never understood how they all knew how to stay close to home without fences or anything, but I guess it's just a country thing.

Now you have arrived. This spot here is where all the action is. Between Aunt Estelle's and Grandma Flossie's, there are two hog pens and two henhouses (with too many hens to count but only two roosters), probably eight or so cats, around five dogs, four hogs, a grapevine, some peach trees, some fields, a garden, some sheds, and about five old cars. This is how I remember it.

We always used to arrive in the middle of the night for some reason. There's nothing like a clear, starry summer night in the country. The air is so clear; you tend to take huge gulps of it without even trying. It's better than any "country fresh" scent anyone has attempted to bottle or can. Normally, we'd drop my sister Erika off at Aunt Estelle's house (that's pronounced "Ainstell," if you didn't know) with her yellow blanket. They had something between them that the rest of us didn't have, although I think it could have to do with the fact that Aunt Estelle let Erika have her cup of coffee in the morning and didn't think her strange for picking all of the raisins out of her raisin bran.

When we arrived, I'm pretty sure that Aunt Estelle was asleep in the rocking chair. From what I recall, she slept there often—rocking and tapping her foot, but asleep nonetheless. I always wondered if she might stay there all night if no one was there to wake her. That picture is how Aunt Estelle stays alive in my mind. She also always had sweets and baked goods. Because we were always around for my birthday, all I ever wanted was some of her precious caramel cake. It may not have been any special secret recipe, but it was the finest golden cake I ever put in my mouth. I'm sure others would agree with me.

When we arrived at Grandma's house, no matter the time, she always had a meal ready for us. Maybe something just needed heating up. Thinking back on it, that's how she was. She had plenty of visitors, but no one ever left her house hungry. My Grandma Flossie was a strong black woman. My fondest, most vivid memory of her is as follows.

Just after daybreak, when the farm was still moist, she would go mix up the hogs' breakfast and feed them. This may seem an odd memory, but picture it: She had to be near seventy at the time, with her yard shoes and old housedress on, with a bucket in each hand. I'm not talking about a little lunch pail, either; these were five-gallon buckets, not bothering her a bit. Remember?

When we visited, the morning was always my favorite time. Erika was still at Aunt Estelle's, so I had Grandma all to myself. We fed all the animals, and then she would make us breakfast. If there were a lot of family visiting, all the women were in the kitchen cooking. Everyone had something to do. Someone might be peeling apples, someone making the eggs, and someone cooking something on the woodstove. I don't know how it felt to everyone else, but to me, it was like a party. Always so much going on.

While some people cooked, others bathed. With just the one bathroom, you might find someone shaving on the back porch, or ironing in the living room, or even bathing over at Aunt Estelle's house. Everyone ate in shifts. I think the unspoken rule was if you slept in, you had to cook your own breakfast. We got spoiled pretty well down in Prospect, I think. I've heard that once upon a time, the farm life at Route 1, Box 162, wasn't so easy. I feel blessed that I came up in a time when I had nothing but fun times and good memories there. From what I understand, at some point, us kids just got bored with it and didn't want to go down to the country to spend our summers anymore. If only I had known then what I know now, I would have realized it was paradise.

I must include a small disclaimer. These are my memories; I realize that this story could be a lot more in-depth. There are many good people and situations I did not include, but this is a brief story, just meant to invoke some fond memories of your own.

Happy Holidays, 2004

Robyn A. Thirkill

Sketch by Joseph Gabbard

Facing Reality: Teen Turns Personal Crisis into Opportunity – February 1992

By Robyn A. Thirkill for The Hyphen – February 1992

"Hey kid, where are you going?"

"I'm going crazy, and don't ever call me 'kid.'"

–Flush Twice Comic and Joke of the Day

I was a rebel… thirteen years old, and I knew everything.

I was so cool.

Hanging out with older kids, drinking, smoking, stealing cars, getting kicked out of school, and feeling no remorse.

I thought I hated my parents, my school, and my life, so I took the car and left forever. Until I met up with a light pole about thirty miles from home.

Two weeks after the car accident, my parents came home and told me to pack. They were taking me to the Psychiatric Institute of Washington.

"No way," I thought. "These couldn't be the parents that spoiled me, got me whatever I wanted, and never told me 'no!'" These perpetrators were putting me in a "loony bin."

Putting on my "don't care" act, I quietly gathered my clothes. The drive to the hospital was the longest three hours of my life. Of course, I had my thoughts to keep me company, but even they were turning on me.

I anticipated a nice little rubber room and straitjacket waiting for me. I was scared to death, but I didn't show it. My parents made light conversation between themselves, but they said not a single syllable to me.

I walked in, trying to look tough. I had my dad's seabag slung over my shoulder, my denim jacket with the big "Anarchy" symbol on the back, and my old ratty Converse All-Stars.

Boy, was I tough, right?

My parents and I had a preliminary meeting with the counselors/intake staff before we went upstairs to Adolescent Psychiatric Unit One ("APU1" to the residents). It all sounded so scary, but I was resilient; I could take anything.

Accidentally, I met my dad's eyes. They looked as pained as I felt.

"If you love me, then why are you doing this?!" I wanted to scream.

My first sight of what was to be my "new home" was a shock. I met lots of young, friendly staff members.

The unit itself was a long hallway with eight bedrooms—four on either side—with two bathrooms and showers at the end. The floor was carpeted, and the walls were colorful. To my surprise, the whole place looked almost normal. Maybe it was just deceiving me.

I was shown to a lounge where ten or eleven teenagers were having some kind of meeting. They were all dressed normally and looked the same as any other kids I might meet. They ranged in age from thirteen to nineteen years.

They introduced themselves and explained why they were there. Then it was my turn. Taking a deep breath, I uniformly stated my name, age, and told them that I didn't know why I was there.

They looked on in utter disbelief.

That night as I was lying on my bed, questions hurtled into my brain: "What am I doing here? What is going to happen to me? Why is this happening?"

At 6:00 a.m., I was awakened by a staff member pounding on my door and yelling: "First wake-up call!"

Still half asleep, I slowly looked around.

"This is real," I thought. "I'm still here."

I got up and looked out the Plexiglass window. The playground below looked quite normal if you overlooked the ten-foot fence topped with barbed wire surrounding it.

I kept to myself most of that first day. I didn't talk much in the groups that seemed to come about once every two hours, and as much as people tried to be friendly toward me, I couldn't find it in me to be friendly back.

After about a week or so, the place began to feel like home. We joked around with each other as if we'd been friends for years. I never thought that I could trust someone I'd only known for such a short time. I never thought that I could trust anyone at all, for that matter. Of course, the place had its bad points, too. I missed my family. Yes, I mean the same people I thought I hated just a few short weeks ago. Being away made me realize how much I loved them.

I also missed my friends. What did they think of me now? Then there were the groups. People made me talk about things that I needed to talk about but didn't want to. The other residents cared about me and wanted to help me get out.

In my thirty-seven days as a "PI kid," I learned more than I ever could in school. What I saw scared me—teens my age and younger who were drug addicts, people who were so depressed that they cried every night, and some who were so emotionally disturbed that they wanted to take their lives.

This was no attention plea; it was real. I decided that I wouldn't end up that way. Yes, I had problems. I was depressed, rebellious, and had trouble in school, among other things.　　But I had a family that loved me. Someone cared.

The people I met at PIW changed my life. I walked out of that hospital with the same seabag slung over my shoulder, the same denim jacket, the same All-Stars.

But I was different.

My eyes were opened to what I didn't want to see before. My life—my great life. Full of love and kindness. It took me thirty-seven days to find it, but I walked out of that hospital with my heart.

Sometimes I think about the kids I met that summer. I owe them my life. I wonder if they've found theirs yet. I wonder if they ever will.

Hangin' with Mr. Cooper

By Robyn A. Thirkill for *The Hyphen*

Making a difference doesn't take experience. At the age of three, I made a difference.

On my family's return trip from London, England, the place of my birth, it was necessary to take a trip to my grandmother's house. She lived in a small town in southern Virginia, where she ran a farm.

For some time now, a man named Cooper had been living with my grandmother to help with the farm work, because all her children had moved away.

None of the visiting children liked Mr. Cooper. They felt he disrespected their mother and had even less respect for them.

Much to everyone's dismay, I took an immediate liking to the old man. Every time he'd prepare to go anywhere, I'd look up at him with begging eyes and wait for the resounding, "Come on, rabbit."

I followed him everywhere, through the cornfield, up the old dirt road, and through the woods to the pond. Whenever I got tired, he'd just pick me up. I'd be asleep before we got to the house.

On the day we planned our drive home, everyone stood on the porch while the men loaded the car. Hugs, kisses, and promises to "see you on the next trip" were expressed.

No one ever said anything to Mr. Cooper. He just stood with his head bowed, occasionally spitting tobacco juice over the railing.

As my dad started to lift me into the car, I broke away.

"C'mon, Mista Cooper," I cried and held out my arms to him. As his eyes turned toward me, everyone stopped.

"Come on, rabbit," he said as he gently picked me up.

If I had looked up, I would have seen tears streaming slowly down his face. Everyone on the porch fought the same feeling. From this moment, there was no more disrespect associated with Mr. Cooper.

When I was eight, Mr. Cooper died of a heart attack. I think I made a difference in those last five years of his life. But he, too, made a difference. In me.

In loving memory: Cooper Patterson, 1983

SOURCE

Baker, Donald P, "Shame of a Nation: The Lessons and Legacy of Prince Edward County

School Closing." *Washington Post Magazine*, March 4, 2001, W08-W017.

Daniel, Jere, "Learning to Love Growing Old" *Psychology Today Magazine*.

https://www.psychologytoday.com/us/articles/199409/learning-love-growing-old

September 1, 1994

Davis v County School Board, 103 F Supp. 337 (E.D. Va. 1952) https://supreme.justia.com

Griffin v School Board 377 U.S. 219 (1964) https://supreme.justia.com

Hershman, J. H., Jr. Massive Resistance. (2011, June 29). In *Encyclopedia Virginia*. Retrieved from http://www.EncyclopediaVirginia.org/Massive_Resistance.

Irons, Peter, *Jim Crow's Children, The Broken Promise of the Brown Decision,* Penguin Books, 2002 Reprint 2007.

Robinson, Scott, "*Aldrena & Mykhayla Thirkill*" photo In Washington Post Magazine,

November 5,2006, www.scottrobinsonvisuals.com

Wikipedia contributors, "Southern Manifesto," *Wikipedia, The Free Encyclopedia,*

https://en.wikipedia.org/w/index.php?title=Southern_Manifesto&oldid=840047531